Anonymus

Bishop Lightfoot

Anonymus

Bishop Lightfoot

ISBN/EAN: 9783743341739

Manufactured in Europe, USA, Canada, Australia, Japa

Cover: Foto ©ninafisch / pixelio.de

Manufactured and distributed by brebook publishing software (www.brebook.com)

Anonymus

Bishop Lightfoot

BISHOP LIGHTFOOT

Reprinted from the QUARTERLY REVIEW

WITH A PREFATORY NOTE

BY

BROOKE FOSS WESTCOTT, D.D., D.C.L.,
Bishop of Durham.

London
MACMILLAN AND CO.
AND NEW YORK
1894

MANY persons having asked for a reprint of this article, Mr. Murray has been good enough to allow it to be made. More than one of those who knew the Bishop best have kindly read it with a view to revision. Special thanks are due to the Archbishop of Canterbury and the Bishop of Durham, both of whom have made valuable suggestions, the latter of whom has also added a prefatory note. It would ill requite their kindness if it were not made clear that neither is responsible for anything except that for which his authority is expressly given. Some passages which pressure of space caused to be omitted from the Review, have been added; but no attempt has been made to occupy the ground of a memoir. This is simply a sketch, not a portrait, though now less unworthy than it was—for artists have touched it—of the great scholar, teacher, bishop, man, whom it seeks to present.

An Appendix contains the Bishop's views on "The Threefold Ministry," extracted by himself from his writings at the close of the Lambeth Conference in 1888.

December, 1893.

PREFATORY NOTE

ALL the friends of Bishop Lightfoot must be grateful to Mr. Murray for allowing the striking sketch of the Bishop's character and work which appeared in the *Quarterly Review* in January, 1893, to be republished separately. Though the writer has not thought fit to reveal himself, it is clear that he had exceptional advantages for fulfilling the task which he undertook ; and the description of the life in Durham shows throughout personal and intimate knowledge. Though my own intercourse with the Bishop during this period was necessarily less close and continuous than during earlier years, I recognise the student, the colleague, the friend whom I knew at Cambridge in every trait, but presented, so to speak, on a larger scale; and I can well believe that while Dr. Lightfoot loved his College and his University with perfect devotion, the busy episcopate, full of great designs and great achievements, was his happiest time. Cambridge, as I often said to him, seemed to be forgotten, and wisely forgotten, in the new interests of Durham; and even I, who was the chief loser, felt that I could rejoice in a greater gain.

In Bishop Lightfoot's case the works were the man. What he did was a true expression of himself; and if I may venture to speak from my experience during the last three years, I believe that his greatest work was the brotherhood of clergy whom he called to labour with him in the Diocese, and bear his spirit to another generation—greater than his masterpieces of interpretation and criticism, greater than his masterpieces of masculine and yet passionate eloquence. I could wish indeed that there was some adequate record of his part in University affairs. When I returned to Cambridge in 1870 I found him possessed of commanding influence, trusted and revered alike by all. But from that time he withdrew more and more from public business, though his authority was never found to be less when he was pleased to use it. If he could persuade another to take up what he had prepared, that seemed to be his chief delight.

I have often spoken of the circumstances which attended my own recall to Cambridge; and perhaps I may repeat the story here, for I think that it reveals the man. As soon as it was known that the Regius Professorship of Divinity would shortly become vacant, he bade me lose no time in arranging for my candidature. I naturally replied that the office was his by right: that his past work led up to it by universal consent: that I might then aspire to be his successor as Hulsean Professor. He acknowledged the force of what I said, "but" he added, "I could not retain my fellowship with it, and that consideration is decisive: I must not give up my place on the Governing Body of the College." I could not resist the argument, so in due time I was appointed. About three months after Dr. Lightfoot came to my rooms and put in my hands a very remarkable letter from Mr. Gladstone containing the offer of the Canonry at St. Paul's. "What could be better," I said, "if it were possible? But, unhappily you cannot hold your fellowship with it." "Ah," he replied, and I can see now his merry smile at my discomfiture, "I have done all I can for the College."

Bishop Lightfoot's works, I have said, show what he was, and this sketch seems to me to add just those touches of life which give to his writings a personal interest. It tells a stranger how he grew and moved among his fellows and won them, and, from a stranger, makes him also in some sense a friend.

B. F. DUNELM.

Auckland Castle,
    October 11, 1893.

1. *St. Paul's Epistle to the Galatians.* By Joseph Barber Lightfoot, D.D., D.C.L., LL.D. London, 1865. Tenth edition, 1892.
2. *St. Paul's Epistle to the Philippians.* By the Same. London, 1868. Tenth edition, 1891.
3. *St. Clement of Rome.* By the Same. London, 1869. Second edition, 1890.
4. *Fresh Revision of the English New Testament.* By the Same. London, 1871. Third edition, 1891.
5. *St. Paul's Epistle to the Colossians.* By the Same. London, 1875. Third edition, 1890.
6. *St. Clement of Rome. Appendix.* By the Same. London, 1877.
7. *Primary Charge.* By the Same. London, 1882.
8. *Charge.* By the Same. London, 1886.

9. *Apostolic Fathers.* Part II. (vols. i.–iii.). By the Same. London, 1885–89.
10. *Essays on Supernatural Religion.* By the Same. London, 1889.
11. *Apostolic Fathers.* Part I. (vols. i. and ii.). By the Same. London, 1890.
12. *Leaders in the Northern Church.* By the Same. London, 1890. Second edition, 1892.
13. *Ordination Addresses.* By the Same. London, 1890. Second edition, 1891.
14. *Cambridge Sermons.* By the Same. London, 1890.
15. *Apostolic Fathers Abridged.* By the Same. London, 1891.
16. *Sermons preached in St. Paul's.* By the Same. London, 1891.
17. *Special Sermons.* By the Same. London, 1891.
18. *Dissertations on the Apostolic Age.* By the Same. London, 1892.
19. *Biblical Essays.* By the Same. London 1893.

BISHOP LIGHTFOOT

"✠ IN MEMORIAM JOSEPHI BARBER LIGHTFOOT S.T.P. EPISCOPI DUNELMENSIS NATUS A.D. MDCCCXXVIII. OBIIT A.D. MDCCCLXXXIX. QUALIS FUERIT ANTIQUITATIS INVESTIGATOR EVANGELII INTERPRES ECCLESIÆ RECTOR TESTANTUR OPERA UT ÆQUALIBUS ITA POSTERIS PROFUTURA ✠ AD MAJORĒ DEI GLORIĀ. AM. PON. CVR. ✠"

SUCH is the inscription encircling the monument which was disclosed to view in the Cathedral Church of Durham on Thursday, the twentieth day of October, 1892, when, in the presence of the Lord Chancellor of England, the Archbishop of the Province, the Bishop of the Diocese, the Speaker of the House of Commons, and a large congregation of dignitaries and commoners of all classes, lay as well as clerical, the Lord-Lieutenant of the county unveiled the effigy of the late Bishop Lightfoot. The monument itself is said to be in every way worthy of the place near the sanctuary which has been assigned to it, of the great prelate whom it commemorates, and of the great artists who devoted to it of their best. Sir Edgar Boehm is known to have worked at the model in the last hours of his life, and Mr. Gilbert has generously completed the unfinished task with a result which reflects honour alike on his master and on himself. It is not, however, with the monument but with the thoughts which the inscription suggests that we propose to deal. It is said to have come from the hand of Bishop Lightfoot's friend and successor, and may be intended to indicate that, as while he was with us so now that he has been taken from us, the retiring man is to be known only by his works. We have seen no announcement of any forthcoming biography, but we cannot help thinking that to a large circle of readers some presentation of the main facts of this great life would be welcome; and in the absence of a fuller record we believe that such a brief sketch as the limits of an article can afford will not be unacceptable. We shall find the chief lines of this sketch in the Bishop's works; but let us look for a moment at the boy who was father to the man.

Joseph Barber Lightfoot was the younger son of Mr. John Jackson Lightfoot, a Liverpool accountant, and was born at his father's house, 84 Duke Street, in that city, on April 13th, 1828. His mother was a sister of Mr. Joseph Vincent Barber, a Birmingham artist of considerable repute, who had married the only daughter of Zaccheus Walker, eldest son of the "wonderful" Walker of Seathwaite, who is immortalised in Wordsworth's *Excursion*. Of the three other children an elder brother became a good Cambridge scholar, and was for many years Master of the Grammar School at Basingstoke. The younger brother was indebted to him for many acts of kindness which removed difficulties from his early course. One sister was married to the Rev. William Harrison, of Pontesbury, and left an only son, who is a curate in the Diocese of Durham. The other survives, and is the only Lightfoot of this branch now remaining. It has been not unnatural to seek to establish a connexion between this family and that of Dr. John Lightfoot, the seventeenth-century theologian and Hebraist, but there is, we believe, no true ground for doing so.

The young 'Joe,' as he was familiarly called at home and at school, was a delicate lad, and was privately educated until he was about thirteen. His first year of school life was under the care of Dr. Iliff, at the Royal Institution in Liverpool, which claims also among its distinguished pupils Dr. Sylvester the mathematician and the present Bishop of Ripon. He soon found his way to the "First Class," which consisted of boys far beyond his own years, and among the more or less legendary stories which have gathered around the early boyhood—such as "How is Joe getting on with his German?" "Oh! he has finished German! he is now doing Anglo-Saxon"[1]—one stands out on clear evidence. The boy's health gave way, and under medical advice the anxious and now widowed mother had all books removed from his room. The little patient grew rapidly worse, and pleaded so earnestly for his books that the mother's heart could not refuse to grant them. They naturally proved the best tonic for the restless mind, and the lad grew as rapidly better.

But the chief step in the boy's education was taken in 1844, when the mother, attracted by the advantages of

[1] *Contemporary Review*, Feb. 1890, p. 174

the Birmingham Grammar School, determined to move to the neighbourhood of her relatives in that town. The picture of the great High Master, Dr. Prince Lee, afterwards first Bishop of Manchester, surrounded by his group of brilliant pupils, has often been drawn, and we must look at it only in connexion with our immediate subject. The streams of influence which have flowed from this centre have, however, been so important in their effect upon our subject and upon the history of religious thought and action during the last and the present generations, that we must for a while place ourselves at the feet of this great teacher. "Three boys," it has been said, "Prince Lee loved more than any one else in the world," and of one of them of whom we are now writing, he is reported to have said, in the winter of 1869, a few days before his own death, "I should like to live to lay my hands on Lightfoot's head once more." Each of the three became a great teacher, and each has given a record of the way in which he was himself taught, which has all the strength of the experience of minds that have had not many equals either as learners or as teachers.[1]

Among the words in which the late Bishop of Durham has himself testified to the influence of Dr. Prince Lee are the following :—

"I have sometimes thought that, if I were allowed to live one hour only of my past life

---

[1] *Cf.* "Memorial Sermon on the Right Rev. James Prince Lee," by Edward White Benson. 1870.

over again, I would choose a Butler lesson under Lee. His rare eloquence was never more remarkable than during these lessons. I have heard many great speakers and preachers since, but I do not recollect anything comparable in its kind to his oratory, when, leaning back in his chair and folding his gown about him, he would break off at some idea suggested by the text, and pour forth an uninterrupted flood of eloquence for half an hour or more, the thought keeping pace with the expression all the while, and the whole marked by a sustained elevation of tone which entranced even the idlest and most careless among us. I suppose that it was this singular combination of intellectual vigour and devotional feeling which created his influence over the character of his pupils.

"Hesitation in all its forms was alien alike to his nature and to his principles. When I wrote to him, stating my intention of taking orders, but representing myself as undecided what branch of the ministry to follow out, he replied characteristically, 'beseeching' me 'to decide *at once: at once* to seek a curacy or a mastership,' if I looked to practical work in either line; '*at once* to begin to read and edit or write,' if I looked to theology; 'for' he added, '*Virtus in agendo constat.*'"[1]

Such was the master who sent from a school small and undistinguished as compared with our present great public schools, five Senior Classics and eight Fellows of his own beloved Trinity in a period of nine years, and of whose thirteen First Class-men twelve became clergymen. Such were the powers which in master and in pupil moulded and throughout his life influenced the character and the work of Joseph Barber Lightfoot.

The Cambridge life commenced in October, 1847, when Lightfoot went up to Trinity and was placed on Thompson's side.[2] From the end of his first year he read with his old

[1] *Ibid. Memorial Notes*, pp. 40, 41.
[2] Afterwards Master.

schoolfellow Westcott, who had preceded him to Trinity, and was Senior Classic in 1848. He obtained a Trinity scholarship in 1849, and though he is said to have been some way behind in the University scholarship examinations, his steady devotion to work and his great development of power placed him easily first in the Tripos, and men talked commonly of papers which had not been equalled and were absolutely free from mistake. In addition to being Senior Classic of his year (1851) he was thirtieth wrangler and first Chancellor's medallist. A Fellowship of Trinity came naturally in the following year, and the Norrisian Prize was gained in 1853. It was gained but not claimed, for with characteristic modesty he was dissatisfied with an essay which the examiners had decided to be first, and he never fulfilled the condition of publishing it. In 1854 the young Fellow was ordained by his old master, Dr. Prince Lee, who had now become Bishop of Manchester, at St. John's Church, Heaton Mersey. In February, 1857, when only twenty-eight years of age, he became Tutor of the College. The impression left upon his pupils is told by such words as these, which some of them have furnished :—

"As a tutor, he was very shy, but gave assurance by his ways of readiness to help. One was certain of strong and kind assistance if one needed it."

"Lightfoot never made any one ashamed of asking him questions."

"He looked round at his pupils, longing for one of them to give him a chance of being kind to him, helping him out in an effort at conversation or advising him. But his temperament did not let him often take the initiative in seeking out and seizing hold of those who wanted help, restraint, or encouragement. He did not thrust his arms out to them, but stood with open arms for those who would come to him."

"As a private tutor he had a singular power of inspiring us with a belief in the duty and the pleasure of hard work, not so much by his brilliance, but by letting us know that his great attainments had been won by sheer diligence. At the same time he was full of humour, and ready to join in any excursion; and he never lost sight of a pupil."

"To have known him in those lighter moods [of reading parties] is a possession for a lifetime." [1]

During the early years of the Trinity Fellowship the four volumes of the *Journal of Classical and Sacred Philology*

[1] See *Cambridge Review*, Jan. 16th, 1890, p. 135.

appeared (1854-9), and they contained frequent contributions from the pen of Mr. Lightfoot, who was one of the founders and editors. Now he writes a minute criticism of the editions of *Hyperides*;[1] now short notices of Schaff's *History of the Apostolic Church*, and of Falkener's "A Description of some important Theatres and other Remains in Crete ;[2] now an article on "The Mission of Titus to the Corinthians ;"[3] now notes on Müller's *Denkmäler der Alten Kunst*,[4] or Webster and Wilkinson's Greek Testament,[5] or the translations of the American Bible Union ;[6] and in immediate contiguity with these last, a notice of Mr. Blew's *Agamemnon*.[7] To the

[1] Vol. i. pp. 109-124.
[2] Vol. ii. pp. 119, 120.
[3] *Ibid.* pp. 194-205.
[4] *Ibid.* pp. 240 *seq*
[5] *Ibid.* pp. 360 *seq*.
[6] *Ibid.* pp. 361-363.
[7] *Ibid.* pp. 363, 364.

third volume he contributes, two months before his election to the Tutorship, the remarkable article on "Recent Editions of St. Paul's Epistles,"[1] a review of Paley's edition of *Æschylus*,[2] and another article "On the Style and Character of the Epistle to the Galatians."[3] The fourth volume contains articles from the same hand on "They that are of Cæsar's household,"[4] "On some corrupt and obscure passages in the Helena of Euripides,"[5] "On the Long Walls at Athens,"[6] and a review of Conybeare and Howson's *Life and Epistles of St. Paul*.[7] These exercises of the young giant in the first freshness

---

[1] Vol. iii. pp. 81–121, cf. *infra*, pp. 24 seq.
[2] *Ibid.* p. 238.
[3] *Ibid.* pp. 289–327.
[4] Vol. iv. pp. 57–79.
[5] *Ibid.* pp. 153–186.
[6] *Ibid.* pp. 294–302.
[7] *Ibid.* pp. 107–109.

of his full and free strength are in some respects of permanent value as contributions to their subjects; and they are of special interest both as a harvest of the seed sown by Dr. Prince Lee's teaching, and as themselves seeds to bear a more abundant harvest of developed fruitfulness in Dr. Lightfoot's later work. The unwearied but concealed labour, the investigation of all available sources of information — inscriptions, MSS., topography—the minute acquaintance with the literature of the subjects, foreign as well as English, the exact scholarship present everywhere and felt especially in emendations of texts, the firm grasp of the laws of language and the laws of mind, the wide outlook on the whole field, the very choice of the subjects, at once recall the schoolroom at Birmingham, and foreshadow the *magna opera* of the life. He is already entering on the field in which he is to gain such marked eminence. *Qualis fuerit antiquitatis investigator, evangelii interpres*—even these works do testify.

The ease with which the writer passes in these articles from one subject to another, from a review of commentaries on St. Paul's Epistles to an emendation of the text of Euripides, from an investigation of the meaning of "Cæsar's household" to the position of the "Long Walls at Athens," represents the work of the Senior Classic and Private Tutor, who at the same time, in the spirit of his own early lessons, regards the New Testament as the goal of all his studies. These articles created so profound an impression in the University that when a vacancy occurred in the Hulsean Professorship of Divinity in 1860, many of Mr. Lightfoot's friends earnestly hoped that he might be appointed to the Chair. He consented at their entreaty to become a candidate, but he felt it was natural that one who, as he modestly said, had done much more for the interpretation of the New Testament than himself should be selected. At the same time the decision seemed to him to bring with it another decision. The time had come for his studies to concentrate and shape themselves in a definite form. The Orestean trilogy of Æschylus had fascinated him as it has fascinated many great minds. <u>He resolved that night to edit it.</u> Some progress was made in this work, when in 1861 the Hulsean Chair was again vacated, and Mr. Lightfoot was chosen to fill it. We regard this selection as one of the turning-points not only in the history of the University of Cambridge, but also in the wider history of Christianity in this country, and from this country throughout the world. Few persons with competent knowledge will be disposed, we think, to challenge this opinion. If any are, we invite them to compare the attendance on the Divinity Professor's Lectures before and after this appointment; to consider the influence on Cambridge life and work of the movements initiated by the young Professor himself, developed later on in union with his friends Dr. Westcott (who returned to Cambridge in 1870) and Dr. Hort[1] who joined them in 1872), and carried into their present

[1] Since this article was in type, a sketch of Bishop Lightfoot's life from the pen of Dr.

state of progress by the band of younger men whom they gathered round themselves; to estimate the effect on English thought of the works enumerated at the head of this article, and of the band of men who have gone forth year by year touched by the spirit and power of the living man who wrote them; to think of this Cambridge movement having its true source in the constant appeal to the Biblical writings as the correlative of the Oxford movement of an earlier generation, and of its sobering effect upon the agitated state of theological thought.

"When he became a Professor at Cambridge," writes one of Dr. Lightfoot's pupils, "his great-

---

Hort, has appeared in the *Dictionary of National Biography;* and, alas! obituary notices of Dr. Hort himself have appeared in the current magazines.

ness was immediately established. The immense range of his acquisitions, the earnest efforts to do his work as well as lay in his power, were at once recognized by the Undergraduates. The frequent failure of Professors to win an audience is a matter of common complaint, and men as learned in their own domain as Dr. Lightfoot have not succeeded. But there was something electric in his quick sympathy with the young, in his masculine independence in his strong practical good sense, in his matchless lucidity of exposition; and these gifts caused his lecture-room to be thronged by eager listeners. The late Master of Trinity was not given to enthusiasm, but once he did wax enthusiastic, as he described to me the passage between the Senate House and Caius College 'black with the fluttering gowns of students' hurrying to imbibe, in the Professor's class-room, a knowledge of the New Testament such as was not open to their less happy predecessors, and such as would last many of them all their lives as a fountain of valuable exegesis in many a parish and many a pulpit." [1]

[1] *Contemporary Review*, Feb. 1890, p. 175.

Among the subjects of the earlier courses of the Professor's lectures was the Gospel according to St. John, and he for some time thought of publishing an edition of this Gospel, an intention which he abandoned only when he found it was entertained by one whom he considered more competent to carry it into effect.

But in the beginning of the year 1865, that is, within four years of his appointment to the Professorship, Dr. Lightfoot published his edition of *St. Paul's Epistle to the Galatians.* Eight years before he had intimated in the article on 'Recent Editions of St. Paul's Epistles,'[1] not only where previous editors had signally failed, both in design and in

[1] *Journal of Philology, ut supra,* vol. iii. pp. 81-121.

execution, but also where they had succeeded, and he thus incidentally discloses what in his own view an edition of St. Paul's Epistles should be.

When the man who had sketched this ideal of a Commentary, and had been afterwards appointed to the Hulsean Professorship, and had delivered courses of lectures which filled the lecture-rooms to overflowing, announced his intention to publish "a complete edition of St. Paul's Epistles," and issued the first instalment of the work, the attention of Biblical students was naturally aroused, and very high expectations were widely formed. We venture to think that no expectation was raised which has not been more than fully realized. The complete plan of the edition has not, indeed, been carried out. It was from the first stated conditionally,—"If my plan is ever carried out,"—and it was so arranged that each part should be complete in itself. We are glad to be able to hope, from hints which have from time to time reached the public ear, that a large portion of the whole field was covered by Dr. Lightfoot's labours, and that some of the MSS. which are in the care of his literary executors will in due course be published; for even if they are only posthumous fragments, the student of St. Paul's Epistles will thankfully welcome them. But the editor's final preparation for the press was given to three volumes only,— the *Galatians*, which appeared in 1865, the *Philippians* in 1868, the *Colossians and Philemon* in 1875; and it is upon these volumes that any claim to have filled the ideal standard which he had himself set for the critic and commentator on St. Paul's Epistles must ultimately rest. The verdict has been given, after most thorough examination, by the most competent judges, and in the most definite form. As each of these volumes appeared it at once took, and has ever since maintained, a recognized position as the standard work on the subject. Grammatical criticism, philological exegesis, historical presentation, philosophical perception, are combined in them as they were never before combined, as they have not been since combined. They have furnished models for others, but they have themselves remained models. With the growth of knowledge in the future they may become obsolete, and some pupil may arise to excel his master ; but the present shows no signs of this, and we may safely predict that any greater commentary on these Epistles of St. Paul will owe part of its greatness to the volumes now before us. It is moreover remarkable as showing the fulness of the editor's early knowledge, and the fixity of his principles, that while edition after edition of these volumes have appeared in quick succession for now many years, they have undergone no material change. The essays reprinted since the author's death, in the volume entitled *Dissertations on the Apostolic Age*, are the essays of the early editions. In one respect important change is here noted. In the earlier editions of the *Philippians* it was assumed in the essay on "The Christian Ministry," that the Syriac version, edited by Cureton, represented the original form of the Epistles of Ignatius. Later and more complete investigations of the writings of this Father, led to the conviction that the shorter Greek form is genuine, and that the Syriac is only an abridgment. An extract from the edition of *The Apostolic Fathers*, to which we shall presently refer, is now added, giving full reasons for the change of opinion. A full note on another subject does not, indeed, express any change of opinion, but protests against imputations of opinion which Dr. Lightfoot never held, and which are inconsistent with a fair interpretation of his essay as a whole. It is not easy to see how an essay which contained from the first such passages as these,

"The evidence for the early and wide extension of episcopacy throughout proconsular

Asia, the scene of St. John's latest labours, may be considered irrefragable."[1]

"If the preceding investigation be substantially correct, the three-fold ministry can be traced to Apostolic direction; and short of an express statement we can possess no better assurance of a Divine appointment or at least a Divine sanction."[2]

could be interpreted as in favour of the Presbyterian as opposed to the Episcopal view of the Christian ministry. But it was natural that controversialists should endeavour to support their arguments by the authority of so great a man; and as advocates will always select their facts, we cannot think it is a matter of surprise that some of the statements have been

---

[1] *Philippians*, p. 212, first edition; p. 214, later edition.

[2] *Ibid.* p. 265, first edition; p. 267, later edition. Cf. *Dissertations on the Apostolic Age*, pp. 239–246.

used, perhaps even understood, in a sense which is opposed to that of the author. A great writer on such a subject is sure to be misunderstood if to be misunderstood is possible, and he should take care to make it impossible. When the sixth edition of the *Philippians* was published, in 1881, the Preface contained the following explanation :—

"But on the other hand, while disclaiming any change in my opinions, I desire equally to disclaim the representations of those opinions which have been put forward in some quarters. The object of the Essay was an investigation into the origin of the Christian Ministry. The result has been a confirmation of the statement in the English Ordinal, 'It is evident unto all men diligently reading the Holy Scripture and ancient authors that from the Apostles' time there have been these orders of Ministers in Christ's Church, Bishops, Priests, and Deacons.' But I was scrupulously anxious not to overstate the evidence in any case; and it would seem that partial and qualifying statements, prompted by this anxiety, have assumed undue proportions in the minds of some readers, who have emphasized them to the neglect of the general drift of the Essay."

Even after this statement the misrepresentations continued, and soon after the close of the Lambeth Conference of 1888, Bishop Lightfoot felt it to be his duty to collect and print a series of extracts from his published writings bearing on this subject. There is nothing new in them. Their value is that they show distinctly what the author's opinion was and had been throughout; and that they were collected by himself. His trustees have done good service in reprinting them[1] together with the Essay and the

[1] To make them easily accessible they are also reprinted at the end of this volume, pp. 129–139.

following note :—" It is felt by those who have the best means of knowing that he would himself have wished the collection to stand together simply as his reply to the constant imputation to him of opinions for which writers wished to claim his support without any justification."[1] It is perhaps hardly to be expected that such misrepresentations will cease, but every vestige of justification, if any ever existed, is now removed.

We have been led by the fact that these editions of the *Epistles of St. Paul* could be regarded only as part of one whole to anticipate some of the events of Dr. Lightfoot's life, and it will be convenient to depart further from chronological order so that we may have

[1] *Dissertations on the Apostolic Age*, 1892, pp. 241–246.

such a connected view of his literary work as is possible within the scope of this article.

Between the date of the *Philippians* (1868) and the *Colossians* (1875) are to be placed the first editions of the *St. Clement* in 1869, and the *Revision of the New Testament* in 1871. Each of these volumes represents the beginning of a stream which flowed on and gathered force until it became an important river.

The *Clement* was the first-fruits of Dr. Lightfoot's studies of the sub-apostolic age, which were afterwards to yield such an abundant harvest. In 1877 followed an Appendix, giving the chief results of the discoveries by Bryennios and Prof. Bensly. Meanwhile much of the editor's attention had been given to a contemplated edition of *Ignatius*, for some portions of this work were already in print, and the "whole of the commentary on the genuine epistles of Ignatius, and the introduction and texts of the Ignatian Acts of Martyrdom .... were passed through the press before the end of 1878." Dr. Lightfoot was called early in 1879 to undertake the manifold responsibilities of the See of Durham. "For weeks, and sometimes for months together," he tells us, "I have not found time to write a single line." But he snatched minutes from his days of work and travel, and hours from his days and nights of rest, and it was at length published in 1885.

We invited the attention of the readers of this Review to the importance of this great work at the time,[1] and we must now limit ourselves to a few words of comment. These shall be the words of Professor Harnack of Berlin, which are of the greater interest as he writes in part from an opposite camp :—

" . . . his [Dr. Lightfoot's] edition of the Epistles of Ignatius and Polycarp, for the appearance of which we have been earnestly looking, and which we now hail with delight. We may say, without exaggeration, that this work is the most learned and careful Patristic monograph which has appeared in the nineteenth century; that it has been elaborated with a diligence and knowledge of the subject which show that Lighfoot has made himself master of this department, and placed himself beyond the reach of any rival."[2]

---

[1] *Quarterly Review*, April, 1886, pp. 467-500.

[2] *Expositor*, December, 1885, p. 1. Cf. Harnack's still more remarkable testimony to Dr.

These three bulky volumes were no sooner out of hand than the editor returned to the *Clement* with the intention of supplying introductions and essays which should place it in form and matter on a level with what were intended to be the companion volumes of *Ignatius*. He devoted to this work hours that many of his friends felt were robbing the Church of his life, but as with the early days,[1] so with the last, his books were really his strength, and up to and during his final illness, as long as consciousness lasted, the *Clement* was constantly in his hands. The second edition of the work was published after

Lightfoot's absolute fairness as distinguished from the tendency of German writers, in *Theologische Literaturzeitung*, No. 12, 1890, col. 298.

[1] *Supra*, p. 8.

his death. It is not as complete as he would have made it, but, to use the language of another great teacher, who, if he writes from the same camp, writes also with fulness of knowledge and exactitude of balanced judgment :—

" .... in spite of some gaps, the book was substantially finished before the end came. He was happily allowed to treat of 'Clement the Doctor,' 'Ignatius the Martyr,' 'Polycarp the Elder,' in a manner answering to his own noble ideal; and the 'Complete Edition of the Apostolic Fathers,' such as he had designed more than thirty years before, was ready at his death to be a monument of learning, sagacity, and judgment unsurpassed in the present age. . . . and in breadth and thoroughness of treatment, in vigour and independence, in suggestiveness and fertility of resource, this new edition of Clement will justly rank beside the 'monumental edition' of 'Ignatius.' "[1]

---

[1] Bishop Westcott, in *Clement*, prefatory note, p. vi.

The Bishop had also made considerable progress with an edition of the *Apostolic Fathers*, in one volume, which was intended for the use of students. He had himself studied some of them in his own school-days in the edition of Jacobson, and he wished to leave as a legacy to the young an edition which should be more complete than any which had yet appeared. This he was enabled to do by the assistance of his friend and chaplain, Mr. Harmer, whose services as general editor the trustees have been fortunate enough to secure since the Bishop's death.

But in the opinion of Dr. Lightfoot the *Ignatius* was the *magnum opus* of his patristic studies, and indeed of his life. This he tells us, " was the motive, and is the core, of the whole."[1] He was not unaware that in the prosecution of this work he was necessarily breaking through another, and, as many thought, a still more important plan.

"I have been reproached" he writes, "by my friends for allowing myself to be diverted from the more congenial task of commenting on St. Paul's Epistles; but the importance of the position seemed to me to justify the expenditure of much time and labour in 'repairing a breach' not indeed in 'the House of the Lord' itself, but in the immediately outlying buildings."[2]

Nor did he overrate the importance of the position. It was nothing less than the chief foundation of the Tübingen school. "To the disciples of Baur," as he expresses it in terms which are not

---

[1] *Ignatius*, preface, p. ix.   [2] *Ibid.* p. xv.

too strong, " the rejection of the Ignatian Epistles is an absolute necessity of their theological position. The ground would otherwise be withdrawn from under them, and their reconstruction of early Christian history would fall in ruins on their heads." [1]

There are probably many of the Bishop's friends who still hold the opinion that nothing can compensate for the interruption of the cherished plan of a complete edition of St. Paul's Epistles. What would they not give for a commentary on the " Romans " and the " Ephesians," on a scale commensurate with those on the " Galatians " and the " Colossians "? With much of this feeling all students of the New Testament will have the deepest sym-

[1] Preface, pp. xi. xii.

pathy, but we are nevertheless of the opinion that the obligations which the Bishop has conferred upon the Church are still greater than they would have been if he had confined himself to a narrower course which he might have completed. It is now with the Pauline Epistles as with the works of the writers of the second century, as with a wished-for opportunity of writing the history of the fourth century, as with many a line of thought, and with many a course of action—if he has not done all he intended, he has at least shown how it should be done.[1] He has left the legacy of an ideal greater even than the actual which he made so great.

[1] *Cf.* Bishop Westcott, *From Strength to Strength*, p. 47.

The *Fresh Revision of the English New Testament* had its origin in a paper read before a clerical meeting just before the Company appointed for the Revision held its first sitting, and it had beyond question a considerable effect both upon the work of the Revisers and upon the attitude of the public towards that work. Among the criticisms which it drew forth was one by Mr. Earle, afterwards Professor of Anglo-Saxon in the University of Oxford, which attacked what Dr. Lightfoot considered to be the impregnable position of his book. He had "laid it down as a rule (subject of course to special exceptions) that, when the same word occurs in the same context in the original, it should be rendered by the same equivalent in the Version." He had indeed laid down the same rule in one of his early criticisms.[1] Mr. Earle in opposing this principle, cleverly described it as substituting the "fidelity of a lexicon" for the "faithfulness of a translation," and Dr. Lightfoot, while regarding this as a misinterpretation of his principle, replied, "My objection to the variety of rendering which Mr. Earle advocates is that it does depart from 'the faithfulness of a translation,' and substitutes, not indeed the fidelity of a lexicon, but the caprice of a translator."[2] Dr. Lightfoot's reply was generally admitted to have established the principle—and indeed, as stated by him, it can hardly

[1] *Journal of Philology*, vol. ii. p. 362.
[2] Preface to the second edition, 1891, p. xii.

be questioned, and yet the Revised Version must have often recalled Mr. Earle's phrase, "the fidelity of a lexicon," which is said, we know not how truly, to have been varied by a learned scholar, who retired from the work of revision on the ground that he had been invited to "translate," and was expected to "construe."

To discuss the merits or demerits of the Revised Version is no part of our present subject, and the readers of this Review are not likely to have forgotten the very full and plain-speaking criticism which has already occupied its pages.[1] Nor have we any available means of determining the extent of Dr. Lightfoot's influence on the work. The history of the deliberations of

[1] *Quarterly Review*, vol. 152, pp. 307 *seq.*; and vol. 153, pp. 1 *seq.*, and pp. 309 *seq.*

the Revisers has not been written, and will probably never be fully known, but the glimpses afforded by Dr. Newth and others of the method of voting are not very encouraging when we think of the inequality of the voters. Surely here, if anywhere, was there place for the principle that votes should be weighed and not counted. It does not appear that Dr. Lightfoot was immediately concerned in the formation of the Company of Revisers, nor was he at the time a member of the Convocation of either Province; but it is clear that from the first nomination of the Company he was among its chief leaders; that he was consistently loyal to his colleagues, and that he was always ready to defend their common work. Perhaps indeed the most uncertain of his contests was that in which he undertook to defend against Canon Cook the rendering, "Deliver us from the evil one." The fresh investigations of Mr. Chase[1] go far in our opinion to confirm the view which Dr. Lightfoot championed, but our readers will remember that there is much to be said on the other side,[2] and we can but regret that Dr. Lightfoot himself did not supply a further reply to Canon Cook's arguments. But while the advocates of the Revised Version are fully justified in claiming Dr. Lightfoot's strong support, we cannot help thinking that if he and a small body of men of like gifts and like knowledge of

---

[1] *Cambridge Texts and Studies*, No. 3: "The Lord's Prayer in the early Church."

[2] *Quarterly Review*, vol. 154, p. 338.

English as well as of Greek had formed the Company of Revisers, we should have now had a version practically accepted by the English-speaking peoples. It is impossible to read the notes in Dr. Lightfoot's editions of the *Epistles of St. Paul* without feeling that we are in a different atmosphere from that of the Revised Version, and we believe that if the Version is to gain general acceptance it will have to be again revised on the more conservative model of the work of the Revisers of the Old Testament. If that task is ever attempted, the new Revisers will find no more fitting words to express their principle than these which Mr. Lightfoot wrote as early as 1857:—

"If, then, the English of former times speaks more plainly to the heart than the English of the present day, and at least as plainly to the understanding, surely we should do well to retain it, only lopping off a very few archaisms, not because they are not *à la mode*, but because they would not be generally understood." [1]

Except indeed in the third of "The Fundamental Resolutions adopted by the Convocation of Canterbury on the third and fifth days of May, 1870:"—

"That in the above resolutions we do not contemplate any new translation of the Bible, or any alteration of the language, except where in the judgement of the most competent scholars such change is necessary." [2]

During the early years of the work of revision Dr. Lightfoot was engaged also upon literary work of another

[1] *Journal of Philology*, vol. iv. p. 108.
[2] *Cf.* Preface of Revised Version of the New Testament.

kind. In 1874 a writer, whose name has never been authoritatively disclosed, but is widely known, published a work entitled *Supernatural Religion: an Inquiry into the reality of Divine Revelation.* He professed to show that there is no miraculous element in Christianity; that miracles are indeed antecedently incredible; that the evidence which is obtainable from the apostolic period is not trustworthy; and that the Four Gospels have no sufficient warrant for their date and authorship. Many reasons combined to give the work an unmerited notoriety, the chief of them being its anonymity and the widely circulated but wholly unwarranted rumour that the author was one of the most learned and venerable of the English prelates. Dr

Lightfoot was led to examine the work publicly, not because of its merits or importance—he thought indeed "that its criticisms were too loose and pretentious, and too full of errors, to produce any permanent effect"—but because he "found that a cruel and unjustifiable assault was made on a very dear friend to whom" he "was attached by the most sacred personal and theological ties." This accounts for a certain tone of severity which is never undeserved, but is present here only in the course of Dr. Lightfoot's writings. The first part of the examination appeared in the *Contemporary Review* in December, 1874; the last in the same periodical in May, 1877. The whole covers to a considerable extent—and the author had intended that it should completely cover—" the testimony of the first two centuries to the New Testament Scriptures;" and it is in our opinion not too much to assert that if the author of *Supernatural Religion* had been the cause of no other investigation than the remarkable articles by Dr. Lightfoot, he would have been the indirect means of contributing the most valuable addition to apologetic literature which has been made during this generation. There was naturally a strong desire in many quarters that the articles should be collected and published in a permanent form. Year after year this was postponed because the writer designed further additions to them, and it was only in 1889, when "life was hanging on a slender thread," that the collection was issued. We could wish indeed that the designed completion had been made, we could wish that the author had been able to abandon the polemical form and to recast the whole; but no course remained but that which has been followed. The work is a legacy as from a death-bed, and it is a legacy of permanent value.

The limits of our space forbid us to refer at greater length to Bishop Lightfoot's literary work, the extent and variety and quality of which would have been remarkable even in a life of learned leisure. Here we have an article or rather the most complete treatise which is known to us on "Eusebius" in the *Dictionary of Christian Biography*; here a similar treatise on the "Acts of the Apostles" in the recently published edition of the *Dictionary of the Bible;* here, courses of lectures on " Christian Life in the Second and Third Centuries" and " Christianity and Paganism" delivered at St. Paul's Cathedral; here, a speech at a meeting of the Society for the Propagation of the Gospel, which has become a standard authority on "The Comparative Progress of Ancient and Modern Missions;" here, an edition of Dean Mansel's treatise on *The Gnostic Heresies;* here, lectures delivered to artisans at Rochdale or students at Edinburgh on "Simon de Montfort and Edward I." or "The Architecture of the Period and the University life, with special reference to Roger Bacon;" now it is the Inaugural Address to the British Archæological Association; now it is that of the President of the Co-operative Society. Here there is the formal "Charge" delivered to his Clergy; here, the address on some public or diocesan question which formed part of his daily work. All are marked by the same characteristic features. The matter is everywhere that of the painful investigator, the principle is that of the Christian philosopher, the form is that of the artist in words.[1]

[1] We have not space to attempt to form a complete bibliography, but reference may also be made to articles in the *Dictionary of the Bible*, 1863, on Romans and Thessalonians; in the *Journal of Philology*, 1868, i. 98, ii. 47, 157, 1869 ii. 204, 1871, iii. 193; in the *Academy*, 1869, Oct. 9th and Nov. 19th, on Renan's *St. Paul*, 1889, May 21st, on *The Lost Catalogue of Hegesippus*, 1889, Sept. 21st, *The Muratorian Fragment;* also notes to the posthumous fragment "Antioch" in Neale's *Holy Eastern Church*,

But the four volumes of sermons mentioned at the head of this article claim at least some words of notice. Archbishop Tait, when walking with a friend one morning, said, "We have made Lightfoot a preacher;" and when asked to explain the process by which such preachers were made, added, "We have given the finest pulpit in the world to a man to whom God has given the power to use it," and expressed his conviction that better use of it had never been made. What Canon Lightfoot himself thought of the opportunity may be read in the dedication of his *Ignatius*:—

1873; a contribution to Scrivener's *Introduction to the Criticism of the New Testament*, 1873, on *The Egyptian or Coptic Versions*; and a lecture on 'Donne, the Poet-Preacher' in *Classic Preachers of the English Church*, 1877.

"To Henry Parry Liddon, D.D., to whom God has given special gifts as a Christian Preacher and matched the gifts with the opportunities, assigning to him his place, beneath the great dome of St. Paul's, the centre of the world's concourse"; and what use he made of it is to be seen in part in the volumes before us. We confess that they have taken us by surprise, and we think that our surprise will be shared by many who often heard Dr. Lightfoot preach and were fully impressed by his sermons. Very rarely have we known sermons which were so good to hear prove so much better to read. We shall not quote from them, because no quotations could adequately represent them. We commend them to any of our readers into whose hands they have not fallen, as models of what sermons should be. They are learned, they are philosophical, they are wide in grasp and firm in tread; but from first to last of these four volumes there is not a passage which is technical and not a sentence which the ordinary reader cannot understand. Their logical clearness satisfies the highest intellect, their deep pathos moves the humblest soul.

It was of course obvious that a man of Dr. Lightfoot's remarkable gifts, and still more remarkable devotion in the use of those gifts, should appear to many persons to be specially qualified to hold many offices, and from time to time offers of preferment were made to him; but his heart was in the work of his professorship, and no suggested honour was acceptable to him which would in any way interfere with the most complete discharge of the duties of that office. He became naturally a select preacher at his own University, and also at Oxford and at Whitehall. He was appointed Chaplain to the Prince Consort, Honorary Chaplain to the Queen, and Deputy Clerk of the Closet. He was for seventeen years Examining Chaplain to Dr. Tait as Bishop of London and Archbishop of Canterbury. But the canonry of St. Paul's was accepted with much hesitation, and only when it was seen that arrangements could be made for his London "residence" which would not break in upon the Cambridge terms. When the Regius Professorship of Divinity fell vacant, in 1870, he practically declined it, in order that he might bring

Mr. Westcott back to Cambridge,[1] but in 1875 he was elected to the Lady Margaret Chair. More than one Deanery, more than one Bishopric, were offered to him on the advice of more than one Prime Minister. In 1879 came the offer of the See of Durham, which, after much hesitation and much pressure from friends, he at length, and with great diffidence, accepted. He was trembling beneath the conviction that he was not fitted for the work to which nevertheless, after

---

[1] "He called me to Cambridge to occupy a place which was his own by right; and having done this he spared no pains to secure for his colleague favourable opportunities for action while he himself withdrew in some sense from the position which he had long virtually occupied." (B. F. Dunelm, in prefatory note to *Clement*.)

prayer and counsel, he felt that he was called of God; the Church was giving thanks for a decision which all men felt to be the dawn of a bright day. For more than two centuries there had been no direct nomination to the throne of the Prince Bishops of Durham, and yet such was the public estimation in which Dr. Lightfoot was held that there was probably no Churchman who did not rejoice in this nomination, except Dr. Lightfoot himself, and a band of Cambridge friends, who thought the loss to the University would be irreparable. There have always been men who thought their own circle was greater than the world.

We now enter upon the last period of Dr. Lightfoot's work, and it is a period in which we trace the signs of an eminence which is higher even than that of his earlier course. Great he was as *antiquitatis investigator*, great he was as *evangelii interpres*, and yet greater when he united and applied the principles and continued the studies of his earlier life in the practical work of the *ecclesiæ rector*. And here, too, *qualis fuerit. . . . testantur opera ut æqualibus ita posteris profutura.*

Dr. Lightfoot was consecrated in Westminster Abbey on St. Mark's Day, 1879, and one sentence in the sermon, which was preached by Dr. Westcott, at once linked together the three old schoolfellows and re-stated for the Bishop then to be consecrated, the principle which his own heart had dictated for the third of the friends exactly two years before. *Who is sufficient for these things?* was the preacher's and yet more the listener's question. The answer now given at Westminster had been given at St. Paul's when Dr. Lightfoot occupied the pulpit, and Dr. Benson was consecrated to be the first Bishop of Truro:—"He who lays down at the footstool of God his successes and his failures, his hopes and his fears, his knowledge and his ignorance, his weakness and his strength, his misgivings and his confidences—all that he is and all that he might be—content to take up thence just that which God shall give him."[1]

The new Bishop was enthroned, the first instance of this ceremony being

---

[1] *From Strength to Strength*, pp. 17, 18.

performed in the person of any Bishop of Durham since the enthronement of Bishop Trevor in 1752, and preached in his Cathedral Church on the 15th day of May. The first words strike at once the dominant note of his life :—

"And what more seasonable prayer can you offer for him who addresses you now, at this the most momentous crisis of his life, than that he—the latest successor of Butler—may enter upon the duties of his high and responsible office in the same spirit; that the realization of this great idea, the realization of this great fact, may be the constant effort of his life; that glimpses of the invisible Righteousness, of the invisible Grace, of the invisible Glory, may be vouchsafed to him; and that the Eternal Presence, thus haunting him night and day, may rebuke, may deter, may guide, may strengthen, may comfort, may illumine, may consecrate and subdue the feeble and wayward impulses of his own heart to God's holy will and purpose!"

The same sermon indicates two of the immediate objects which the preacher set before himself. One is the division of the Diocese, the other is the duty of the Church in social and industrial questions.[1]

In such devotion, such resolves, such stating and strengthening of principles, passed the first day in the Diocese. The succeeding days were forthwith devoted to carrying these principles into practice. The Bishop lived at first in the Castle at Durham, the ancient home of the Prince Bishops, which had become part of the University through the munificence and foresight of Van Mildert, but in which a suite of rooms had been reserved in perpetuity for the Bishop's

[1] *Leaders in the Northern Church*, pp. 164, 165.

use. Here the Visitor of the University was heartily welcomed alike by graduates and students, and these early weeks strengthened the attachment which he brought with him, and laid the foundations of a warm and never broken affection for what he was wont to call the University of his adoption.

It is said that among Dr. Lightfoot's last words to some of his Cambridge friends when he took leave of them was the charge, "Send me up men to the North." As soon as Auckland Castle was ready to receive him, he carried out his cherished project of forming a clergy-house under his own roof. Here a band of University men, seven or eight in number, were trained under his own immediate guidance for their future work in the Diocese. They were instructed by himself, by his archdeacons, and by his chaplains. The intellectual work followed the lines of a college course in theology, the practical work in Auckland itself and the pit villages which encircle the castle-grounds enabled the students to test their theories by the realities of life; but their chief lesson was the constant influence of their true Father in God. We have referred to Dr. Prince Lee's affection for his pupils, and those who know best assert that it is at least equally true that Bishop Lightfoot loved nothing on earth more devotedly than those who were in a special sense his spiritual sons. His strong love strengthened theirs, and men in the vigour of their young manhood learned to love him, and through him to love afresh their God. To love him was to learn from him, to assimilate him, to reproduce him; and not the least of the permanent influences for good which the Bishop left to his Diocese and his Church, was the band of young men numbering more than seventy who had looked upon a life which in the power of its intellect, the devotion of its soul, the humility and self-sacrifice of its whole being was to them a daily ascension into heaven; and who, as they looked upon it had caught something at least of its spirit. Loving them and knowing them as he did, he expected them and always found them to be ready to work with entire singleness of aim and entire devotion to duty. They knew they had no claim to preferment unless to a post of unusual poverty or unusual difficulty, and to such a post only when prepared for it. Some words from an " In Memoriam " sketch in a college magazine and signed J. B. D., will show how the Bishop looked upon his sons and their work, and what manner of men they were :—

" A new district was to be formed in a much-neglected neighbourhood in ——. There was neither church nor endowment nor parochial appliances of any kind. Everything must be built up from the foundation. Only a modest stipend for a single curate-in-charge had been guaranteed. It was necessary to rely on youthful zeal, even at the cost of some inexperience I asked C——, who was still curate at ——, to undertake the task of building up this new parish, and he accepted the call. To my great joy, B—— offered to accompany his friend as a volunteer without remuneration, though he might have had an adequate stipend elsewhere. . . .

" I spoke of this offer then as an inspiration, and so I regard it now. Though doubtless the work there hastened his death, who shall regret his decision? Certainly not those who loved him best. . . .

"I cannot but regard this splendid unselfishness as a chief corner-stone, on which the edifice of the new parish was raised. . . . Excellent congregations were gathered together; generous donors came forward with liberal offerings; and within two years and a few months from the time when they commenced their work in the district, a large and seemly church was finished and consecrated.

"I have had placed in my hands some extracts from a private diary which he kept. . . . I give this relating to the night before his ordination: '*Ἦν διανυκτερεύων ἐν τῇ προσευχῇ τοῦ Θεοῦ.* If He, how much more I needed. So in the end I remained praying in my own room till daylight, about 3.15. It was broad day, and I went to bed.'

"Of the day itself he writes:—

"'Sunday, Matins at 8.15. I felt calm and at peace. . . . Just broke fast and nothing more. I had no fixed idea about fasting, but thought it better to err in too literal a following of the Apostles than too free a departure from them.'

"'The service at South Church was full of a depth of peace and love to me, such as I have never known. The *Veni Creator* began the climax. My heart was full of an overpowering sense of my own unworthiness and Christ's deep love and trust in one who had done nothing but what deserved the withdrawal of love and trust; and at the actual imposition of hands the surge of mingled regrets and hopes, joys and fears, the sense of being at once infinitely humbled and exalted, broke out *in lacrimas super ora surgentes [et] defluentes. Gaudebam, quia contristabar; contristabar, quia gaudebam.*'"

The Bishop adds, "A ministry" [may we not add, "an episcopacy"?] "so supported, could not be otherwise than fruitful."

With this sketch drawn from the sanctuary of the home life at Auckland

Castle, it will be interesting to compare a *pendant* drawn from without. Among the guests entertained by the Bishop in 1882 was the Rev. Robert W. Barbour, a gifted young Free Church Minister. From a memorial volume printed for private circulation after his early death, which shows what a loss this brought to his church and his friends, we are permitted to print the following extracts:—

April 28, 1882.

. . . .

"10.45.—The evening worship was very uniting. The servants came in, and we sang the psalms and hymns, and Dr. Lighfoot and a chaplain read and prayed (from the new version and the prayer book) in his own voice and with his own devout, simple soul uttering itself in all. His after talk in the drawing-room was even more charming [than that in the afternoon]. You know how a mastiff will lie down (out of sheer love for the canine race) and let a crowd of small dogs jump and tumble over him, and put them off, and egg them on with great pawings and immense 'laps' of his broad tongue. Even so did Dr. Lightfoot. .... It is good for me to be in the midst of so much informal earnestness and Christian manliness."

April 29, 1882.

. . . .

"Then I suppose it is not taking her past out of the hands of time, to say that Butler's seat is now filled by his nearest successor; a man as great in his work and in his day, as his great namesake (for they both are written 'Joseph Dunelm'). I know not if there be any better test of true lastingness in any man who is yet living, than when, knowing his written works, one is able to compare them with his person, and to say that these correspond. The same judgment which you admire in Dr. Lightfoot's commentaries meets you in his conversation. He seems, like justice in her statues, always to give his sentences, holding meantime a pair of other scales. Indeed, the analogy might be extended. Justice is but badly described in stone as being blind-folded in her decisions. But there is in the Bishop a strong cast of eye which enables him, when he speaks, to address himself to nobody in particular; although immediately after speaking, he turns on you a glance that conveys an impression of the most absolute impartiality. . . . He calls these lads (and I can imagine worse things than to feel myself, for the nonce, one of them) his family, and they treat him as frank, ingenuous English gentlemen's sons would treat their father. He is accessible to their difficulties and their doubts, if they have any; but, a thing more remarkable, he is open to all their kittenhood of mirth and fun. To hear him alone with them is to feel you are on the edge of a circle, which tempts you almost to stand on tiptoe and look over and wish you were inside. It is a searching trial of true homeliness, to observe how it comports itself when there are strangers present. But I assert my coming in has not bated one jot of all this family joy. Last evening, after prayers, they were poking fun at the bishop. One man was asked how he was getting on with Hebrew. The fellow boldly turned the weapon round by inquiring whether his lordship was prepared to teach him. Dr. Lightfoot was gently demurring, when somebody else burst in, as if with a child's impatience and fear of some older imcompleted promise: 'No, not before we have had these lectures on botany.' Then, assuming the air of someone to whom that study was even as his necessary food, he went on to report his observations, taken daily on his walks to and from the district, of two *interesting weeds*. It sounded like a clever parody upon Darwin and his climbing plants trained up the bed-post. I have written all this in order to show—if it is within the power of words to show a thing which lies more in the feeling of the whole, than in any enumeration, however complete, of the details—how happy an example one has here of the spirit and the action of the English Church. Within, you have a home and a beehive both in one; without everything is plain, and simple, and strenuous. The Bishop preaches such sermons as the one I sent you. His chaplains teach, and visit, and preach. The students an earnest, and healthy set of men. Nothing is allowed in the Castle which speaks of pomp or pretension. You go down morning and evening to prayers in the chapel; I suppose it is about the finest palace chapel in Britain. A simple service is held. The Bishop and a chaplain read the lessons and lead the prayers. Another chaplain has trained a choir of boys from the neighbouring town. Behind these choristers sit the students; the bishop and servants (eight I counted) are in the back seats. One or two from the outside also seem to attend. The psalms and hymns are simply but sweetly sung. So anxious is Dr. Lightfoot that nothing should be unused, nothing rest in an empty name, that I believe he is fitting up the chapel with seats, so as to have a service every Sabbath. Much of what I have seen here, the earnestness and the manliness of the men, the order of the household, the thoroughness of the instruction, the devoutness of the prayers, the sweetness of the singing, the beauty, the learning, the goodness, the simplicity, make me hang my head for shame, both as a man and as a minister; for my whole heart consents to these things that they are right..."

Arrangements having been made for a supply of living agents for the work of the Diocese, two heavy tasks at once confronted the Bishop; the division of the Diocese, and the provision of additional churches and mission-rooms.

The first of these he had inherited. As long ago as 1876 Bishop Baring had submitted the question to his Ruridecanal Chapters, and "the judgment was almost unanimous as to the advisableness of creating the See." A year later Mr. Thomas Hedley bequeathed the residue of his estate, from which some £17,000 was ultimately realized, as the nucleus of the necessary fund. In 1878 the Act for the creation of the four Sees—Liverpool, Newcastle, Southwell, and Wakefield—was passed, and was characterized by Archbishop Tait as " one of the greatest reforms proposed by the Church of England since the Reformation." Bishop Baring spoke for the last time in the House of Lords in favour of this measure, but he did not regard the Newcastle scheme as one which was likely to be realized at an early date. "The prospect of the accomplishment of this good work is, I fear, far remote," he said in his Charge, which was delivered later in the same year.[1] Soon after Bishop Lightfoot's appointment he had an interview with the Duke of Northumberland, who promised the munificent gift of £10,000 to the fund. The Bishop thereupon pledged himself to use every endeavour to accomplish the scheme; but by the counsel of all competent advisers he for a time withheld his hand. A deep cloud of darkness then hung over the commerce and

[1] See *Guardian*, Jan. 1st, 1890.

industries of the north-eastern counties, and it seemed to be hopeless to ask for subscriptions. In December, 1880, it was possible to organize a committee. Men soon caught what one called the "electric enthusiasm" of the Bishop's ideas, and in nine months the work was practically done. At the Church Congress of 1881, which was held in Newcastle, the Bishop of Manchester appealed for subscriptions to complete the fund, which had reached the critical stage of near accomplishment that is often so difficult to pass. The appeal was liberally answered, but still the last thousands did not come, and the question of a house was becoming an additiona difficulty, when the most happy solution offered itself through the liberality of Mr. J. W. Pease, a member of the

Society of Friends, and a banker in Newcastle. It was on the 15th of October, 1881, that the following letter was received by the Bishop through the then Archdeacon of Northumberland. We quote it as showing both the widespread influence of the Bishop and the noble spirit of the generous donor:—

"DEAR MR. ARCHDEACON,—So many people tell me that Benwell Tower is the most suitable place for the new Bishop that I think you ought to have it. Funds do not come in very quickly, and the purchase of such a house as you require must therefore be a difficulty. This being the case, I have concluded to hand the place over to the Committee, and as it is not occupied, they are very welcome to the possession at once, so that any alterations which may be considered needful may be made without loss of time, and their solicitor can communicate with mine as to the conveyance.

"Churchmen and Quakers used not to get on

very well together, but these times are past, and I most sincerely trust that the important step about to be taken may be in every way successful. What I propose to instruct my solicitor to convey is the Tower, with its garden, old burial-ground, stables and lodge, and as many of the cottages near the stables as you may require. . . . Yours very truly, JOHN PEASE."

This gift was followed by another munificent offering of £10,000, made by Mr. Spencer of Ryton, and by a gift of the furniture for Benwell Tower through a Committee of Ladies. The fund required was thus more than realized, and the task which the Bishop had undertaken was more than accomplished. On St. James's Day, 1882, Dr. Ernest Roland Wilberforce was consecrated in Durham Cathedral as the first Bishop of Newcastle.

When the great work of the division

of the See was accomplished, the Bishop was more free to mature his plans for Church Extension in the county of Durham. Along the banks of the Tyne, the Wear, and the Tees, and in so-called "pit villages," through a large part of the county, new and vast populations had been called into existence by the development of the coal, iron, and shipping industries. A country road, such as that along which the Bishops of Durham had driven from their castle at Auckland to the Cathedral Church, and by the side of which one house stood some fifty years ago, had become for a considerable part of its course a street, with a network of houses on either side. A seaside village, like Stranton, had developed into a great port like Hartlepool. Efforts had been made, and with much success, by former Bishops, and notably by Bishop Baring, to keep pace with this abnormal growth; but the fact remained, and stared Bishop Lightfoot in the face, that in almost every part of his Diocese the church accommodation was far from adequate to the needs of the people. The measure of the people's need was for him the measure of the Church's duty, and the Church's duty was the motive power of his own immediate action. He had learnt to the full both in school and in life that *Virtus in agendo constat.* Cautious men pleaded now that "times were bad," but so they had pleaded before when the Newcastle Bishopric Fund was commenced. There was the added plea that this fund had deeply drained all available resources, but the Bishop's one answer was in effect, " Look at these sheep: as their shepherd I must in the name of God try to provide folds for them, and in the name of God I must call upon you to help me."

In January, 1884, a meeting was held in the Town Hall at Durham under the presidency of the Lord-Lieutenant of the county, for the purpose of hearing from the Bishop a statement of the needs of the Diocese. The Archbishop of York had generously come to help him. The nobility and gentry of the county were well represented, but the meeting was not a large one, for not a few had learned to fear the influence of an address from the Bishop. He pleaded in simple and earnest terms for funds to provide twenty-five churches and mission-rooms which he felt to be urgently needed, and supported his plea by a generous gift. Again the contagion of his enthusiasm and his munificence spread, and a sum approaching £30,000 was subscribed in the room. "Why, the Diocese has gone mad!" said a well-known layman after the meeting; but it was a madness the results of which are now written in deeds for which the most sanguine could not then have hoped, and for which thousands do and will bless God. At the end of five years—and these years a period of deep and continued commercial depression—the Bishop was enabled to report, not that the twenty-five buildings for which he had pleaded were in progress but that "no less than forty-five churches and mission-chapels had been completed, or will shortly be so, through the instrumentality of the fund." Nor did the force of the wave spend itself there or then. It sent its impetus into many parishes, where no immediate work of church-building was needed, and its direct force can be traced to the present day. The Bishop himself offered, in thanksgiving for the completion of the *decennium* of his episcopate, the noble building which probably is the only instance in our own country of a dedication—and in this case a peculiarly appropriate one—to S. Ignatius the Martyr. Another church now being built in the same town of Sunderland owes its existence to his forethought and his gifts, and will be a memorial of his name and work. Gateshead also will, under similar conditions, soon have its Bishop Lightfoot Memorial Church, and these, the two largest towns in the Diocese, are but examples of the spirit and work of the whole.

Another practical scheme to which the

Bishop gave much attention and which was a natural supplement to his Church Building Fund, was a Diocesan Fund. This was intended to form a combination of all the various funds in the Diocese for Churches, Schools, Provision for Insurance and Pensions for the Clergy, and so on, and in addition was to provide a fund under the direction of a representative committee, which should aid any one or more of the allied funds in case of need, and should itself provide for any special work—a mission clergyman here, a parish room there, a temporary endowment in a third place—which may from time to time arise.

"I propose the present effort," wrote the Bishop, "to be wholly different to anything which has preceded it, both in kind and magnitude. It ought not only to supplement existing organizations, but also to plant and to maintain living agents in districts with which the Church would otherwise be unable successfully to deal. In short, as I have said on a previous occasion it will be the handmaid of the Diocese, stepping in at times and places where the need is sorest. Above all, it will teach us to feel the high privilege of acting as members of a great spiritual community, by stepping outside the limits of parochial efforts, and taking a larger conception of our responsibilities."

Here, as in all other cases, his appeal to others was strengthened by his own munificence. Five hundred pounds was the annual subscription which he proposed to contribute personally, and it was natural that the Diocese should support him nobly, as it did. In addition to the large gifts of rich men and the apparently small gifts of poor men, came the annual collections in churches, which were made in all the parishes of the Diocese—with exceptions so few that they do but emphasize the unanimity.

It will seem, perhaps, that more than enough has been written to show how fully the Bishop's time and thought were given to the details of his Diocesan work; but the contents of the two quadrennial Charges which fall within the period of his episcopate are so fully illustrative of this, and at the same time so suggestive, that we cannot refrain from quoting them :—

1882.

I. THE DIOCESE.
    (1) *Territorial Rearrangements.*
        (i) Division of the Diocese.
        (ii) New Archdeaconry.
        (iii) Rearrangement of Rural Deaneries.
        (iv) Subdivision of Parishes.

(2) *Diocesan Institutions and Associations.*
   - (i) Diocesan Conference.
   - (ii) Diocesan Societies.
   - (iii) Organization of Lay Help.
   - (iv) Lay Readers.
   - (v) Ministration of Women.
   - (vi) Girls' Friendly Society and Young Men's Friendly Society.
   - (vii) Diocesan Preachers.

(3) *Miscellaneous.*
   - (i) Ordinations.
   - (ii) Meeting of Curates.
   - (iii) Confirmations.
   - (iv) Church Building and Restoration.
   - (v) Diocesan Calendar and Magazine.

(4) *Retrospective and Prospective.*

II. THE CHURCH.
   (1) *Burial Laws Amendment Act.*
   (2) *Permanent Diaconate.*
   (3) *Salvation Army.*
   (4) *Revised New Testament.*

(5) *Vestments.*
(6) *Church and State.*
(7) *Anxieties and Hopes.*

1886.

I. THE DIOCESE.
   (1) *Church Extension.*
      (i) Churches, Chapels, and Parishes.
      (ii) Cemeteries and Churchyards.
   (2) *The Services.*
      (i) Services in Supplementary Buildings.
      (ii) Holy Communion.
      (iii) Weekday Services.
      (iv) Choirs and Hymns.
      (v) Letting and Appropriation of Pews.
   (3) *The Clergy.*
      (i) Ordinations.
      (ii) Junior Clergy.
      (iii) Increase in the Clergy.
      (iv) Canon Missioner's Work.

(4) *Lay Ministrations.*
    (i) Lay Readers.
    (ii) Lay Evangelists.
    (iii) The Church Army.
(5) *Confirmations.*
(6) *Diocesan Finance.*
    (i) Financial Statement.
    (ii) Collection of Statistics.
    (iii) General Diocesan Fund.
(7) *Diocesan Societies.*
    (i) Church of England Temperance Society.
    (ii) White Cross Army.
    (iii) Girls' Friendly Society.
    (iv) Diocesan Sons of the Clergy.
    (v) Diocesan Board of Inspection.
    (vi) Parochial Schools Society.
    (vii) Diocesan Board of Education.
(8) *Conclusion.*

II. THE CHURCH.
    (1) *Church Patronage.*
    (2) *Church Revenues.*
    (3) *Ecclesiastical Courts.*
    (4) *The Church House.*

These Charges were a cause of disappointment to many of the Bishop's friends. They had hoped that he would follow the example of some other learned men who had been called to Bishops' thrones, and had thence addressed the Church and the world on questions of the day. But he deliberately chose his line. In his opinion :—

"A visitation is a great audit time, when the Bishop and clergy alike render an account of their ministrations—the clergy by their answers to the questions of their diocesan—the Bishop by his charge summing up the work of the diocese during the few years past. It is a foreshadowing and a forecast of the great and final visitation, when the Master Himself returning shall demand an account of His talents, when the Chief Shepherd shall reappear and require His flock at our hands." [1]

---

[1] "Primary Charge," 1882, p. 3.

Not that he failed to feel constantly the pulse of great movements. He never forgot that he was a Bishop of the Anglican Church, but he always remembered that he was the Bishop of Durham. The Church and the wider questions which affect the Church at large have their place in both the Charges, but the Diocese had the primary claim at a visitation of the clergy of the Diocese. And what a picture of the work of a diocese do these Charges give! In almost every detail is there ground for humble thankfulness for the progress of the past, and ground for hopeful counsel for the work of the future. What a picture, too, do we get incidentally of the work of a Bishop!

"I am thankful to say," he writes in 1886, "that there are now only a few churches in my

Diocese in which I have not officiated, and I hope before long to complete the circuit. I have preached "—and the volumes before us tell us of what kind these sermons were—" in all the churches in Gateshead, Darlington, Stockton, and Sunderland (including Bishopwearmouth and Monkwearmouth), and in nearly all in Durham, South Shields, and the Hartlepools—in the principal churches in these towns several times."[1]

Some of the Bishop's friends were also disappointed, and perhaps with more show of reason, that his voice was seldom heard in the House of Lords. But here, too, he was guided by the same principle. He never forgot that he was a lord of Parliament, but he always remembered that he was primarily Bishop of Durham. He was indeed never absent from the House of Lords at a

[1] "Charge," 1886, p. 9.

critical division, though his presence involved the sacrifice of an important Diocesan engagement and two nights in a railway carriage; his counsel was always at the command of the leaders of the Episcopal Bench; no man was more in touch with every movement for the social as well as spiritual welfare of his countrymen; but he naturally did not attach to his own utterances the weight which others did, and he felt that the interests of the Church and the people were most safely guided by the great Archbishops, upon whom this burden naturally fell.

Nor did he shrink, when it came clearly in the path of his own duty, from expressing his opinion or offering his counsel on questions which were of universal interest. In 1881 he presided over the twenty-first meeting—the coming of age—of the Church Congress at Newcastle-on-Tyne. The British Association had just kept its jubilee in the metropolis of the Northern Province. Here is the Bishop's happy and characteristically hopeful reference to the coincidence :—

"The President availed himself of the occasion to sum up the achievements of the half-century past—untrodden fields opened out, fresh sciences created, a whole world of fact and theory discovered, of which men had hardly a suspicion at the beginning of this period. In this commemoration we are reminded of the revolution in the intellectual world which has taken place in our own time, as in the other[1] our attention was directed to the revolution in the social and industrial world.

---

[1] The George Stephenson Centenary, which had been recently observed at Newcastle.

Here again we are confronted with a giant force, of which the Church of Christ must give an account. If we are wise we shall endeavour to understand and to absorb these truths. They are our proper heritage as Christians, for they are manifestations of the Eternal Word, who is also the Head of the Church. They will add breadth and strength and depth to our theology. Before all things we shall learn by the lessons of the past to keep ourselves free from any distrust or dismay. Astronomy once menaced, or was thought to menace, Christianity. Long before we were born the menace had passed away. We found astronomy the sworn ally of religion. The heresy of the fifteenth and sixteenth centuries had become the orthodoxy of the nineteenth. When some years ago an eminent man of science, himself a firm believer, wrote a work throwing doubt on the plurality of worlds, it was received with a storm of adverse criticism, chiefly from Christian teachers, because he ventured to question a theory which three centuries earlier it would have been a shocking heresy to maintain. Geology next entered the lists. We are old enough, many of us, to remember the anxiety and distrust with which its startling announcements were received. This scare, like the other, has passed away. We admire the providential design which through myriads of years prepared the earth by successive gradations of animal and vegetable life for its ultimate destination as the abode of man. Nowhere else do we find more vivid and striking illustrations of the increasing purpose which runs through the ages. . . . Our theological conceptions have been corrected and enlarged by its teaching, but the work of the Church of Christ goes on as before. Geology, like astronomy, is fast becoming our faithful ally. And now, in turn, Biology concentrates the same interests, and excites the same distrusts. Will not history repeat itself? If the time should come when evolution is translated from the region of suggestive theory to the region of acknowledged fact, what then? Will it not carry still further the idea of providential design and order? Will it not reinforce with new and splendid illustrations the magnificent lesson of modern science—complexity of results traced back to simplicity of principles—variety of phenomena issuing from unity of order—the gathering up, as it were, of the threads which connect the universe, in the right hand of the One Eternal Word?

"Thus we are reminded by these two celebrations of the twin giants, the creation of our age, with which the Church of Christ has to reckon—foes only if they are treated as such, but capable of being won as trusty allies, by appreciation, by sympathy, by conciliation and respect."

In 1885 the Bishop presided at a meeting of the Diocesan Conference at Durham. Disestablishment was in the air and to many persons seemed nearer then than it does now. He was led to speak at some length upon it. We extract a few sentences:—

"But I cannot blink facts. The question is not sleeping; it has been definitely raised; and I should hold it culpable in anyone in my position not to express, and express definitely, his opinion on the issues involved. . . . The only schemes which are before us involve a wholesale alienation of property, a disregard of personal and corporate rights, and a violation of all the most sacred associations and feelings, such as, in the words of an eminent living statesman, would leave England "a lacerated and bleeding mass." Of any such scheme of disestablishment I say deliberately, having carefully weighed these words and feeling the tremendous responsibility of over-statement, that it would be not only a national disaster, but also a national crime, to which it would be difficult to find a parallel in the history of England since England became a nation. I believe that a moral blow would be inflicted on this country, under which it would reel and stagger for many generations to come, even if it ever recovered."

In October, 1889, just two months before his death, the Bishop presided over the Conference of his Diocese in Sunderland. He addressed it on many subjects, and especially on the Lambeth

Conference, Christian Socialism, the White Cross Movement, the Brotherhood of the Poor. How touching in the light of what followed, how firm in the strength of faith, is this reference to himself :—

"While I was suffering from overwork, and before I understood the true nature of my complaint, it was the strain, both in London and at home, in connexion with this Pan-Anglican gathering, which broke me down hopelessly. I did not regret it then, and I do not regret it now. I should not have wished to recall the past, even if my illness had been fatal. For what after all is the individual life in the history of the Church? Men may come and men may go—individual lives float down like straws on the surface of the waters till they are lost in the ocean of eternity; but the broad, mighty, rolling stream of the Church itself—the cleansing, purifying, fertilising tide of the River of God—flows on for ever and ever. A gathering of Bishops, so numerous and so representative, collected from all parts of the globe, is an incident quite unique in the history of this Diocese. . . . For to those who have eyes to see and ears to hear, what does it all mean? What activities does it not suggest in the Anglican Church of the present? What capacities and hopes for the Anglican Church of the future? What evidences of present catholicity? What visions of future diffusion? . . . I hold that God has vouchsafed a signal blessing to our generation in this demonstration of the catholicity of the English Church, and I consider myself happy that in my chapel at Auckland will be preserved for future generations a memorial of this chief event of my episcopate."

How full of wisdom is this comment on the work of the Lambeth Conference :—

"But it may be said: this was a very important and very suggestive gathering, but what was the outcome? Did it leave behind any result at all proportionate to the imposing spectacle? What questions did it settle, disposing for ever of the relations between Christianity and science, or between religion and politics or social life—questions of infinite perplexity, which are troubling the minds of men in our own generation?

"Heaven be thanked, it did not lay down any formal dogma or infallible decree on any of these points. There is such a thing as hastening to be wise, even in Church Councils and Conferences. Of all the manifold blessings which God has showered on our English Church, none surely is greater than the providence which has shielded her from premature and authoritative statements, which soon or late must be repudiated or explained away, however great may have been the temptation from time to time. The Church of England is nowhere directly or indirectly committed to the position that the sun goes round the earth; or that this world has only existed for six or seven thousand years; or that the days of creation are days of twenty-four hours each; or that the scriptural genealogies must always be accepted as strict and continuous records of the descent from father to son; or that the sacred books were written in every case by those whose names they bear; or that there is nowhere allegory, which men have commonly mistaken for history. On these and similar points, our Church has been silent; though individuals, even men of high authority, have written hastily and incautiously." [1]

The above extracts are all taken from addresses which the Bishop delivered within the limits of his own Diocese, but it would entirely misrepresent him if the impression should be formed that his sympathies and work were confined to these limits. If space were at our command, we should like to quote other passages, which show how fully he was in touch with the work of the Church far and near. Now he gives an address at meetings of the Church Congress at Leicester and Carlisle; now he preaches

[1] Diocesan Conference, 1889.

the Congress Sermon at Wolverhampton[1]; now and again he crosses the Border to show his warm sympathy with his brethren in Scotland. His voice was constantly heard in London on behalf of this or that philanthropic society; and here and there throughout the country, clergymen whose only claim was their need, asked for and obtained his help. To Cambridge he was bound by many ties, and the series of "Cuddesdon Addresses"[1] shows that to Oxford he was no less generous.

Nor was it in public only that this help was given. Auckland Castle was almost constantly filled, as with the sons

---

[1] We are referring to his work as Bishop. His earlier paper at the Congress at Bath in 1873, and his sermon at Croydon in 1877, are not likely to be forgotten.

[2] *Ordination Addresses*, pp. 214-318.

of the house who were being prepared for their future work, so with the clergy and laity from the Diocese, and from afar, who were welcomed to his hospitality and to his counsel. Few perhaps realize what the burden is which the post-bag adds to a Bishop's daily life, and in his case it brought the scholar's burden too; but even this was cheerfully borne, and no letter remained unanswered, whether it was that of the Southern farmer who wished to know if the Bishop could supply him with Durham cows, or that of a lady who felt sure he could find time to read a theological work in MS. before she sent it to the press—and " may she say in her preface that it had his approval ?"—or that of the student in the far West who had just begun the Greek Testament, and would like a solution of his many difficulties, and had "heard that the Bishop was a good scholar." In small matters, as in great, no one asked for anything which he felt that he could give, and asked in vain. And so, year after year, the hard work was done, and the noble life was lived. The mental and physical strength seemed equal to every strain. No engagement ever fell through, no weariness was ever apparent. *Ignatius* was refreshment from the work of the Diocese: the work of the Diocese was refreshment from *Ignatius*. The face was always bright; the heart was always glad. The happiest years of his life he thought these Durham years to be; and he thought that he had never been so strong. It was towards the close of the spring confirmations in 1888, when the pressure of work had been unusually heavy, and falls of snow had more than once blocked the roads by which he tried to travel, that this strength seemed for the first time to be strained. He thought, and his friends thought, that a short summer holiday would completely restore him; but the Lambeth Conference came and the visit of the Bishops to Durham came. Both brought to him great happiness, but both brought much work. The autumn holiday was too late, and the Bishop returned to his Diocese only to leave it again, under positive medical orders, for a winter in Bournemouth. He at once thought of resigning the Bishopric. It was foreign to his whole thought to have personal interests distinct from his office. He could not conceive that any man could accept an office in the Church of Christ without identifying himself with it, or would hold it a day longer than he could fully discharge its duties. One of the burdens which weighed on his soul was that instances to the contrary were not wholly wanting in his Diocese. He at least would do the one thing which was right. But he was still comparatively young; hopes of restoration to health, and strength, and work, seemed to be well grounded; and those to whom he was bound by every tie of allegiance absolutely forbade the step he wished to take. An Assistant Bishop, first welcomed and soon beloved by himself and by his Diocese, was found in the person of Bishop Sandford, and he somewhat doubtingly acquiesced in a course about which others had no doubt. The spring of 1889 seemed to bring a fulfilment of the hopes which had been formed. The Bishop was able to return to his Diocese, and on Ascension Day the Cathedral Church was crowded by a vast assembly who joined with him in a special Service of Thanksgiving. He was able to fulfil the ordinary Diocesan duties, and to devote a large amount of time to literary work during the months of the summer and autumn; and he took part in three public events of special interest. On July 2nd he consecrated the Church of S. Ignatius the Martyr, Sunderland, his own noble gift of thanksgiving; on October 17th he presided over the Diocesan Conference, and delivered the remarkable address to which we have referred;[1] on October the 29th he received in a public meeting, at the hands of the Lord-Lieu-

---

[1] *Supra,* pp. 102 *seq.*

tenant, the beautiful Pastoral Staff, which, together with a portrait by Mr. Richmond, it was determined to present to him on the completion of the tenth year of his episcopate. He thanked the donors in his usual happy, cheerful, tone, and took his farewell with tender words of blessing. It was for the last time. He left for the purpose of wintering again in Bournemouth a few days afterwards. For a time he continued to make progress. He was able to work regularly at the *Clement* up to Tuesday, December 17th. The local papers of the following Saturday morning contained a note from Archdeacon Watkins, "asking the clergy and other ministers of religion to make special supplication for our beloved Bishop on Sunday and other days." The evening papers of the same day contained a telegram from Bournemouth —" The Bishop of Durham passed peacefully away this afternoon, at a quarter to four o'clock."

The sorrow of the Church and of the nation, and the expression of that sorrow in the pulpit and in the press, is still fresh in the memory. The death and burial [1] were the natural sequence to the life. True goodness and true greatness are honoured by men of every opinion and by men of every rank.

Some estimates of the work of Bishop Lightfoot which were uttered under the influence of strong feeling immediately after death, contained perhaps some expressions and some comparisons which history will not justify. We are writing

[1] See a full account in the *Guardian* of Jan. 1st, 1890.

I

from the vantage-ground of three years' distance, and with access to many papers and references which have been kindly placed at our disposal, and have endeavoured at every point to follow in the spirit of the inscription which has formed our motto: *Qualis fuerit . . . testantur opera.* For this reason we have largely quoted the Bishop's own words, and if we try to express our own estimate of his work we shall still have recourse to words which he used of another, and which with little change may be as truly said of himself :—

"But after making all allowance for the fond partiality of a recent regret, we may fairly say that as a Bishop of Durham he stands out pre-eminent in the long list of twelve centuries; as a man of letters, greatest of all save De Bury; as a restorer of the fabric and order of churches, greatest of all save Cosin; as a profound thinker, greatest of all save Butler; as a munificent and patriotic ruler, greatest of all save Barrington; but as uniting in himself many and varied qualifications which combined go far towards realizing the ideal head of a religious and learned foundation, the just representative of a famous academic body, greater than these or any of his predecessors. Vast and varied mental powers, untiring energy and extensive knowledge, integrity of character and strictness of example, a wide and generous munificence, a keen interest in the progress of the Church and the University, an intense devotion to his own Diocese, a strong sense of duty, a true largeness of heart, a simple Christian faith; the union of these qualities fairly entitles him to the foremost place among the Bishops of Durham."[1]

It is natural that men should have attempted not only to portray this great life, but to analyse it; and the Church and the nation would owe a deep debt of gratitude to the writer who could

[1] Cf. *Cambridge Sermons*, p. 119 (of Dr. Whewell).

show us how in any degree other men can learn the principles, of which the life and character of Joseph Barber Lightfoot were the product. Two statements among the many which lie before us are of special value in themselves, and derive a special interest from the widely-different sources from which they come.

Canon Westcott, preaching in Westminster Abbey two days after the funeral, said :—

"What then, you will ask me, is the secret of the life of him to whom we look this afternoon with reverent regard? It is, in a word, the secret of strength. He was strong by singleness of aim, by resolution, by judgment, by enthusiasm, by sympathy, by devotion. In old days it was strength to be with him: and for the future it will be strength to remember him."[1]

---

[1] *From Strength to Strength*, p. 44.

Lord Durham, speaking on two occasions separated by three years, said:—

"I venture to attribute the success of the Bishop to the strong personal feeling he inspires in all those who know him. It is impossible to have been connected with him or to have come in contact with him, without appreciating his strong sympathy and his generous regard for the welfare of the people surrounding him. ... I think that no prelate in the proud and old princely days of the Palatinate of Durham, with all his pomp and with all his circumstance, ever commanded more true respect than our present Bishop with his simple, kindly life, and his generous and unostentatious charity."[1]

"In every town and parish in this county you will find visible and tangible evidence of his untiring zeal, and of the impetus which his genius gave to all those who served under him. But what you will not see, and what no hand

---

[1] Presentation of Pastoral Staff, October 29th, 1889.

can probe, is the impress he made upon the hearts of all with whom he came into contact, and the softening influence of his genial presence upon all sorts and conditions of men. .... I venture to think that the chief factor in his paramount influence amongst us was his true and genial sympathy—sympathy with our joys and our sorrows, sympathy with our aspirations and with our failures; with our pursuits and with our recreations; and, above all, boundless sympathy with the shortcomings of feeble human nature. He was no proud Pharisee, who thanked God that he was not as other men are, but a true-hearted Christian gentleman, conscious of the trials and temptations of the world, striving with his pure life, and humble, modest ways, to raise mankind to a higher and better level by his example of Christian charity and loving sympathy." [1]

It seems to be certain that the two great secrets of the Bishop's power are here—strength and sympathy. And yet

[1] Unveiling of Monument, October 20th, 1892.

they were veiled in a modesty which men thought amounted to shyness. They were held in reserve; they were ready for fullest use whenever occasion demanded. But his very sympathy was strong, and he could not understand some forms of weakness. One of his early pupils has told us ". . . he was kindness itself. . . . I once offended him . . . by telling him, when I got my Fellowship that he might have saved me many gloomy misgivings as an Undergraduate, if the Cambridge system had dealt a little more freely in words of encouragement."[1] One of his clergy, whom he had placed in several difficult posts, said to another after some years of service, "It would remove a burden from my mind if I felt sure that my work was

[1] *Contemporary Review*, Feb. 1890, p. 174.

being done as he wished it, but he has never said to me a single word of encouragement." The second replied, "I have had a larger experience, but I should never look for such words from him. He expects strong men to do their work, and would as soon think of encouraging such men as of seeking encouragement in words for himself. They must do all and bear all in the light of the Divine Presence, as he himself does." And yet this second speaker received from the Bishop, not long before his death, a note which contained the following words: "I have never ceased to be thankful for the inspiration which led me to invite you to assist me in the work of the Diocese. May God give you every blessing."

Strength and sympathy! But the

secret principle lies deeper still; and here again the Bishop's own words must guide us. The text of his enthronement sermon was "And they shall see His face," and we have already quoted words [1] which tell the secret of which we are in quest. The prayer which from the first he asked his Diocese to offer for him was—

"That the Eternal Presence, thus haunting him night and day, may rebuke, may deter, may guide, may strengthen, may comfort, may illumine, may consecrate and subdue the feeble and wayward impulses of his own heart to God's holy will and purpose!"

The "consciousness of an Eternal Presence"—that was the principle of his life. That made him strong; that made him sympathetic; that gave him

[1] *Supra*, p. 64.

absolute singleness of aim and simplicity of life; that filled him with a buoyant optimism which expressed itself in constant joyousness; that was the source of an almost unparalleled generosity which in life gave to God and the Church every gift which God gave him, and at death made his chaplains his executors, and his Diocese his residuary legatee; that was the strength which nerved the mind to think and the hand to write in the solitary room before the hard day of public life began and after it ended; that was the wondrous power of personality which made itself felt in Cambridge, in London, in Durham, by men of every degree. He was ever conscious of the Eternal Presence. He ever went to men from God, and the human presence was illumined by the Divine.

Did boys at school wonder that Lightfoot never spoke an ignoble word, or did an ignoble deed? The secret finds its explanation in the spirit which led him and a younger schoolfellow, afterwards not less eminent than himself, to arrange a form of prayer for the hours of the day for their common use. Did men marvel at the influence of the young Fellow and Tutor of Trinity? They would have marvelled less had they known that his life was strengthened by the following among other prayers :—

"Since it hath pleased Thee, O Lord, that I should be called to take my part in the teaching of this College, grant that I may not assume the same lightly, or without a due sense of the importance of my trust; but, considering it a stewardship, whereof I shall have to render an account hereafter, may faithfully fulfil the same to Thy honour and glory. Grant, O Lord, that neither by word nor deed I may do aught that may weaken the faith, or slacken the practice of those committed to my charge ; but rather grant to me such measure of Thy Holy Spirit, that my duties may be discharged to Thy honour and glory, and to the welfare of both the teacher and the taught. Grant this, O Lord, through Thy son, Jesus Christ, who is the Way, and the Truth, and the Life. Amen."

Or if they had known that in the pressure of that busy life he found time to write to schoolboys such words as these :—

" Remember me to all the boys. . . . Good-bye. Fight manfully against all school-boy temptations. Be as brave as a lion in defence of all that is good. Strive to live purely and uprightly. Work hard." [1]

---

[1] The letter which contains these words is dated Nov. 1st, 1859. It tells of, among things interesting to a boy, the first companies furnished by Trinity to the Volunteer Rifle Corps, and of a meeting which was to bear rich fruit :— " It

Did peers and pitmen, rich and poor, old and young, in the Diocese of Durham feel that a strange influence of sympathy and strength had come among them and had touched their hearts? Had they followed the great Bishop of Durham to his inner chamber they would have found him resting, for the too few hours he gave to sleep, on a simple iron bedstead which the pitman would have spurned; and they would have seen

is a very busy day with us here. There is a large meeting in the Senate House to provide a mission to central Africa—the regions explored by Dr. Livingstone. The Bishop of Oxford, Mr. W. E. Gladstone and other great speakers are to be there." When the young Trinity Fellow had become Bishop of Durham he welcomed to the Diocese his school-boy friend as organizing secretary of the Universities Mission to Central Africa. "The seed is good."

hanging close by the side of it a simple German engraving of Albert Dürer's *Crucifixion*, with the legend " Es IST VOLLBRACHT."[1]

Among the last words which the Bishop addressed to the public from the very brink of the grave were these :—

"I believe from my heart that the truth which this Gospel [of St. John] more especially enshrines—the truth that Jesus Christ is the very Word incarnate, the manifestation of the Father to mankind—is the one lesson which, duly apprehended, will do more than all our feeble efforts to purify and elevate human life here by imparting to it hope and light and strength, the one study which alone can fitly prepare us for a joyful immortality hereafter."[1]

---

[1] See the sermon on these words (*It is finished*), "The Death of Bede," in *Leaders in the Northern Church*, pp. 87-101.

[1] Published after his death in the *Expositor*, March, 1890, p. 188.

The first words of the *Will and Testament* by which he spoke from beyond the grave, were these :—

"With ever-increasing thankfulness to Almighty God for his many and great mercies vouchsafed to me, hoping to die, as I have striven to live, in the light of God's fatherly goodness as revealed through the Cross of Christ."

Such were the principles of this great life—*Qualis fuerit . . . . testantur opera; qualis fuerit testantur . . . .* FIDES ET PRECES PRIVATÆ.

APPENDIX

See p. 32.

THE THREEFOLD MINISTRY.

(*From the writings of the Bishop of Durham.*)

1. *Commentary on the Epistle to the Philippians* (*Essay on the Christian Ministry*, 1868).

(i) p. 199, ed. 1 : p. 201, later edd.

Unless we have recourse to a sweeping condemnation of received documents, it seems vain to deny that early in the second century the episcopal office was firmly and widely established. Thus during the three decades of the first century, and consequently during the lifetime of the latest surviving Apostle, this change must have been brought about.

K

(ii) p. 212, ed. 1; p. 214, later edd.

The evidence for the early and wide extension of episcopacy throughout proconsular Asia, the scene of St. John's latest labours, may be considered irrefragable.

(iii) p. 235, ed. 1; p. 227, later edd.

But these notices, besides establishing the general prevalence of episcopacy, also throw considerable light on its origin... Above all they establish this result clearly, that its maturer forms are seen first in those regions where the latest surviving Apostles (more especially St. John) fixed their abode, and at a time when its prevalence cannot be dissociated from their influence or their sanction.

(iv) p. 232, ed. 1; p. 234, later edd.

It has been seen that the institution of an episcopate must be placed as far back as the closing years of the first century, and that it cannot, without violence to historical testimony, be dissociated from the name of St. John.

(v) p. 265, ed. 1 ; p. 267, later edd.

If the preceding investigation be substantially correct, the three-fold ministry can be traced to Apostolic direction ; and short of an express statement we can possess no better assurance of a Divine appointment or at least a Divine sanction. If the facts do not allow us to unchurch other Christian communities differently organized, they may at least justify our jealous adhesion to a polity derived from this source.

2. *Commentary on the Epistle to the Philippians (Preface to the Sixth Edition),* 1881.

The present edition is an exact reprint of the preceding one. This statement applies as well to the Essay on the Threefold Ministry, as to the rest of the work. I should not have thought it necessary to be thus explicit, had I not been informed of a rumour that I had found reason to abandon the main opinions expressed in that Essay. There is no foundation for any such report. The only point of importance on which I have modified my views, since the

Essay was first written, is the authentic form of the letters of St. Ignatius. Whereas in the earlier editions of this work I had accepted the three Curetonian letters, I have since been convinced (as stated in later editions) that the seven letters of the Short Greek are genuine. This divergence however does not materially affect the main point at issue, since even the Curetonian letters afford abundant evidence of the spread of episcopacy in the earliest years of the second century.

But on the other hand, while disclaiming any change in my opinions, I desire equally to disclaim the representations of those opinions which have been put forward in some quarters. The object of the Essay was an investigation into the origin of the Christian Ministry. The result has been a confirmation of the statement in the English Ordinal, 'It is evident unto all men diligently reading the Holy Scripture and ancient authors that from the Apostles' time there have been these orders of Ministers in Christ's Church, Bishops, Priests, and Deacons.' But I was scrupulously anxious not to overstate the evidence in any case; and it would seem that partial and qualifying statements, prompted by this anxiety, have assumed undue proportions in the minds of some readers, who have emphasized them to the neglect of the general drift of the Essay.

3. *Sermon preached before the Representative Council of the Scottish Episcopal Church in St. Mary's Church at Glasgow* October 10, 1882.

When I spoke of unity as St. Paul's charge to the Church of Corinth, the thoughts of all present must, I imagine, have fastened on one application of the Apostolic rule which closely concerns yourselves. Episcopal communities in Scotland outside the organization of the Scottish Episcopal Church—this is a spectacle which no one, I imagine, would view with satisfaction in itself, and which only a very urgent necessity could justify. Can such a necessity be pleaded? "One body" as well as "one Spirit," this is the apostolic rule. No natural interpretation can be put on these words which does not recognize the obligation of external, corporate union. Circumstances may prevent the realization of the apostle's conception, but the ideal must be ever present to our aspirations and our prayers. I have reason to believe that this matter lies very near to the hearts of the Scottish Episcopalians. May GOD grant you a speedy accomplishment of your desire. You have the same doctrinal formularies: you acknowledge the same episcopal polity: you respect the same liturgical forms. "Sirs, ye are brethren." Do not strain the conditions of reunion too tightly. I cannot say, for I do not know, what faults or what misunderstandings there may have been on either side in the past. If there have been any faults, forget them. If there exist any misunderstandings, clear them up. "Let the dead past bury its dead."

* * * * * *

While you seek unity among yourselves, you will pray likewise that unity may be restored to your Presbyterian brothers. Not insensible to the special blessings which you yourselves enjoy, clinging tenaciously to the threefold ministry as the completeness of the Apostolic ordinance and the historical backbone of the Church, valuing highly all those sanctities of liturgical office and ecclesiastical season, which, modified from age to age, you have inherited from an almost immemorial past, thanking GOD, but not thanking him in any Pharisaic spirit, that these so many and great privileges are continued to you which others have lost, you will nevertheless shrink, as from the venom of a serpent's fang, from any mean desire that their divisions may be perpetuated in the hope of profiting by their troubles. " Divide et impera " may be a shrewd worldly motto; but coming in contact with spiritual things, it defiles them like pitch. "Pacifica et impera" is the true watchword of the Christian and the Churchman.

4. *Epistles of St. Ignatius*, Vol. I. pp. 376, 377, 1885.

The whole subject has been investigated by me in an Essay on 'The Christian Ministry'; and to this I venture to refer my readers for fuller information. It is there shown, if I mistake not, that though the New Testament itself contains as yet no direct and indisputable notices of a localized episcopate in the Gentile Churches, as distinguished from the moveable episcopate exercised by Timothy in Ephesus and by Titus in Crete, yet there is satisfactory evidence of its development in the latter years of the Apostolic age; that this development was not simultaneous and equal in all parts of Christendom ; that is more especially connected with the name of St. John ; and that in the early years of the second century the episcopate was widely spread and had taken firm root, more especially in Asia Minor and in Syria. If the evidence on which its extension in the regions east of the Ægean at this epoch be resisted, I am at a loss to understand what single fact relating to the history of the Christian Church during the first half of the second century can be regarded as established ; for the testimony in favour of this spread of the episcopate is more abundant and more varied than for any other institution or event during this period, so far as I recollect.

5. *Sermon preached before the Church Congress at Wolverhampton*, October 3, 1887.

But if this charge fails, what shall we say of her isolation ? Is not this isolation, so far as it is true, much more her misfortune than her fault ? Is she to be blamed because she retained a form of Church government which had been handed down in unbroken continuity from the Apostolic times, and thus a line was drawn between her and the reformed Churches of other countries? Is it a reproach to her that she asserted her liberty to cast off the accretions which had gathered about the Apostolic doctrine and practice through long ages, and for this act was repudiated by the Roman Church? But this very position,—call it isolation if you will—which was her reproach in the past, is her hope for the future. She was isolated because she could not consort with either extreme. She was isolated because she stood midway between the two. This central position is her vantage ground, which fits her to be a mediator, wheresoever an occasion of mediation may arise.

But this charge of isolation, if it had any appearance of truth seventy years ago, has lost its force now.

6. *Durham Diocesan Conference. Inaugural Address*, October, 1887.

When I speak of her religious position I refer alike to polity and to doctrine. In both respects the negative, as well as the positive, bearing of her position has to be considered. She has retained the form of Church govern-

L

ment inherited from the Apostolic times, while she has shaken off a yoke, which even in medieval times our fathers found too heavy to bear, and which subsequent developments have rendered tenfold more oppressive. She has remained steadfast in the faith of Nicaea, but she has never compromised herself by any declaration which may entangle her in the meshes of science. The doctrinal inheritance of the past is hers, and the scientific hopes of the future are hers. She is intermediate and she may become mediatorial, when the opportunity occurs. It was this twofold inheritance of doctrine and polity which I had in view, when I spoke of the essentials which could under no circumstances be abandoned. Beyond this, it seems to me that large concessions might be made. Unity is not uniformity. . . . .On the other hand it would be very short-sighted policy—even if it were not traitorous to the truth—to tamper with essentials and thus to imperil our mediatorial vantage ground, for the sake of snatching an immediate increase of numbers.

7. *Address on the Re-opening of the Chapel, Auckland Castle*, August 1st, 1888.

But, while we 'lengthen our cords,' we must 'strengthen our stakes' likewise. Indeed this strengthening of our stakes will alone enable us to lengthen our cords with safety when the storms are howling around us. We cannot afford to sacrifice any portion of the faith once delivered to the saints; we cannot surrender for any immediate advantages the threefold ministry which we have inherited from Apostolic times, and which is the historic backbone of the Church. But neither can we on the other hand return to the fables of medievalism or submit to a yoke which our fathers found too grievous to be borne—a yoke now rendered a hundredfold more oppressive to the mind and conscience, weighted as it is by recent and unwarranted impositions of doctrine.

www.ingramcontent.com/pod-product-compliance
Lightning Source LLC
Chambersburg PA
CBHW030343170426
43202CB00010B/1223